The Whimsical Sage

FOR PARENTS AND TEACHERS AND LOVERS OF
WORDS AT PLAY
FOR ALL AGES

By Michael Sage

Illustrated by Jenny Ross

Publisher
Joan Sage, Philadelphia, PA

Published by Joan Sage
914 Kimball Street
Philadelphia, PA 19147
Library of Congress Control Number: 00-092942
ISBN 0-9669813-1-6

Acknowledgments:

For ideas and support from the following friends
of Joan Sage:

Gene Coladonato and Dave Elser for introducing Joan
to Jenny Ross.

Ken Garland, Library Services Specialist for the School District of
Philadelphia, who has always understood Joan's motivation for
publishing Mike's writings as a tribute to his gifts, intended not as
a commercial venture but as a way to give others another
opportunity to enjoy his books.

Dean Smith • Grisha Zeitlin • Lisa Diantoniis • Anne Cecil •
Anne Cramer • Paula Spielberg • Stephen Thomas Shandor •
Trish Creegan • Lilly Dorsa • Sofia Kostos • Jesse Trbovich at the
Philadelphia Museum of Art • Nancy Heller • Nancy Wright •
Joyce Sabatino • Brian Perpiglia • David Lorenz Winston •
Alex Heston • Elizabeth Endicott-Heston • Mary F. Robinson •
Ellen Goldin • Theresa Smith • Ariel Weiss Holyst •
Richard Kagan • Dr. Steven S. Fries • Gerald D'Alessio, Ph.D. •
Kilian Fritsch, Ph.D • Aurora Deshauteurs

Special thanks to Heather Karasow for her proofreading and calm
guidance throughout the process of producing this book.

Suggestions and support from:

Jenny's mother, Constance Ross, and the following friends of
Jenny: Abby • Brian • Jake • Christian • Bonny • Norman

Text dedicated to 11 year old Amelia Louise Heston
who remembers sharing laughter with Mike when she
was 2 years old and he was 80.

And in memory of that shy delightful book lover
Florence Geismar who defined Mike's writings as "whimsical."

Drawings in loving memory of Jenny's father, Leslie Ross.

Joan Sage is grateful to Jenny Ross for her enthusiasm in
illustrating Mike's words which inspired the dream of creating
this book.

Dictionary definitions of WHIMSICAL:
singular ideas or impulses,
capricious, quaint,
delicately fanciful,
expressing gently humorous
tolerance.

The Whimsical Sage

TABLE OF CONTENTS

DIVERSE VERSES DIVIDE ALL OF THE ABOVE

Dippy Dos and Don'ts

So many things are clear to me

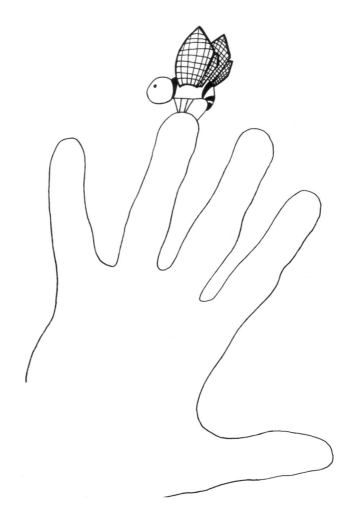

Like never pet a honeybee.

And if your shadow's on a chair

You can't go out and leave it there.

Don't put salt on jelly beans
Or pepper in your tea.

And if you chase a foolish fly
You'll make the fool fly flee.

Potatoes have a lot of eyes,
A clock has hands and face,

A table may have four strong legs
But cannot win a race.

Don't ever grow a long, long nose

Or you will kick it with your toes.

A horse may have a great big throat
But he can't talk of course,

And if you find that you can't talk
You know your throat is hoarse.

A tiger's nice and never rough

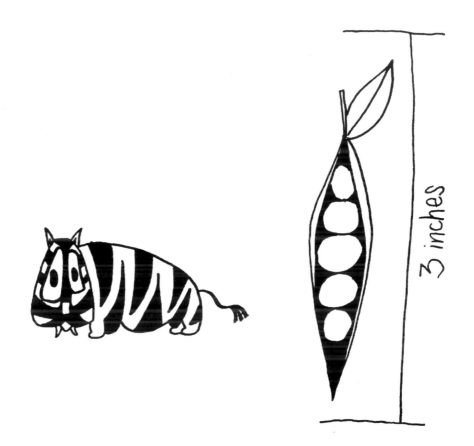

3 inches

But just make sure he's small enough.

Never shake hands with a lobster
is one of Nature's laws.

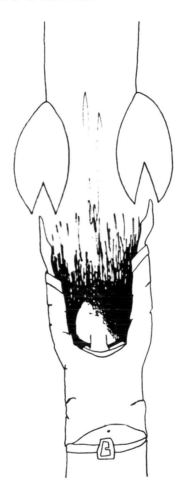

Never shake hands with a lobster
Why? —Oh, just be-claws.

Cookies or a chocolate cake

Are easier to eat than make.

If there is milk inside your cup

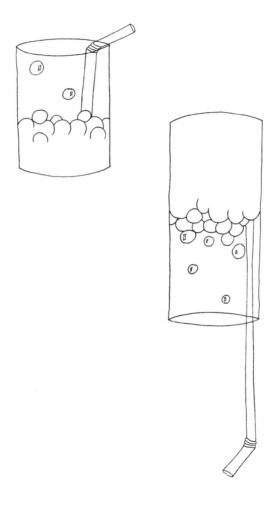

Drink it down—or drink it up.

Don't tell me it's snowing hard
Because I don't agree.

The snow that's falling in my yard
Feels very soft to me.

When you lose your ball
Never mind it.

Losing your temper
Won't help you find it.

A steam roller could press your coat
in a minute.

But it's very much better if you're not in it.

You cannot ever weigh yourself
Upon a fish's scale.

And how a monkey climbs a tree
Is a long, long tail.

Don't play checkers with a frog
It won't be any fun.

He'll be making twenty jumps
While you're just making one.

It's very very impolite

To turn off Mom and kiss the light.

●

Oh, words are funny, words are queer
I'll show you what I mean right here.
For instance, here's a silly trick
That words play with arithmetic:
If you try adding 1 and 1
Your answer's 2—the job is done.
But try your best (you'll see it's true)
You can't make <u>ONE</u> and <u>ONE</u> be <u>TOO</u>!

$$\begin{array}{r} 1 \\ + 1 \\ \hline 2 \end{array}$$

●

Threes are very round and plump
Ones just stand up straight
Fours are much like tic tac toe
And two small o's make eight.

●
A line that's straight's exactly what's
The shortest route between two dots
The lines that curve like paths in parks
Are often designated arcs
Yes, lines are here
And lines are there
And lines are everywhere about
But as for me
Just leave me be
A line I can do without.

Deep In A

Haystack

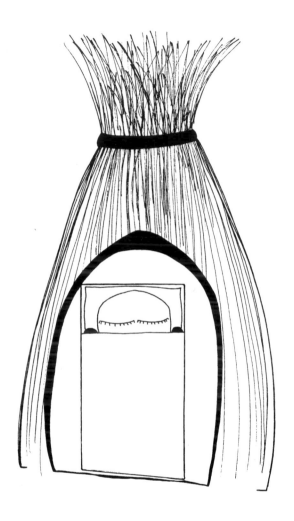

Deep inside a haystack
Sandy was sleeping and dreaming lots of dreams.

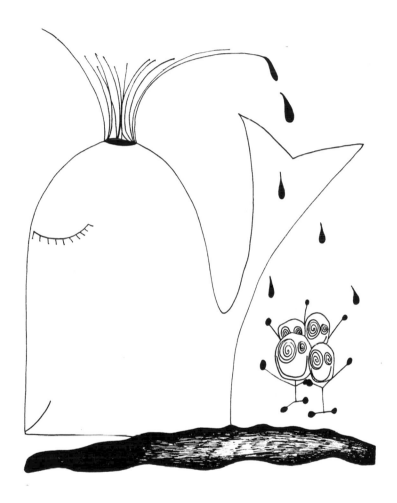

First, Sandy dreamed he was a whale
and made a fountain for the children in the park.

Next he dreamed he was a tiny fish
and could visit all the children
through the faucet in the sink.

Then he became a lion
and his roar was so loud
it made the trees shake.

After that he was a sparrow
and caught any balloon that flew away.

Then he dreamed he was a camel
and children loved to slide down his hump.

And then—a kangaroo
that could jump over any house
or over the moon.

He dreamed he was a hippopotamus
and gave children rides on his back.

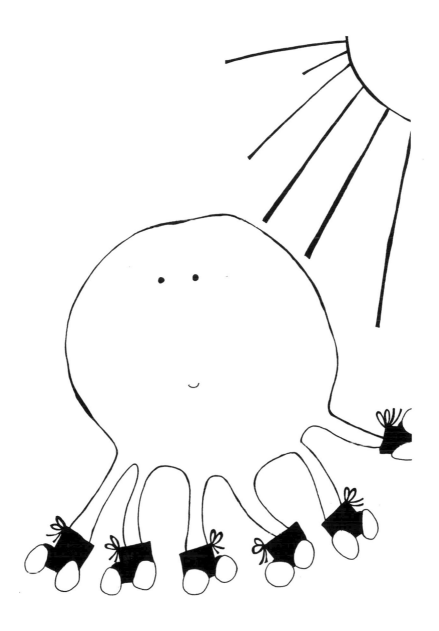

In his next dream he was an octopus
and was the best skater in the park.

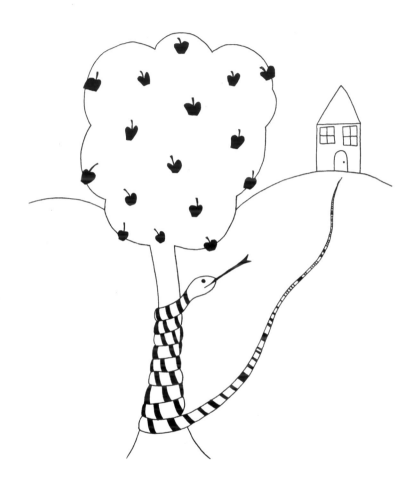

After that he was a long, long snake
and no matter where he went
he was always halfway home.

Sandy dreamed he was a horse
and ran as fast as the wind.

Sandy dreamed he was a giraffe
and could peek into any bird's nest.

And then—a pelican
who always had his bill full of candy.

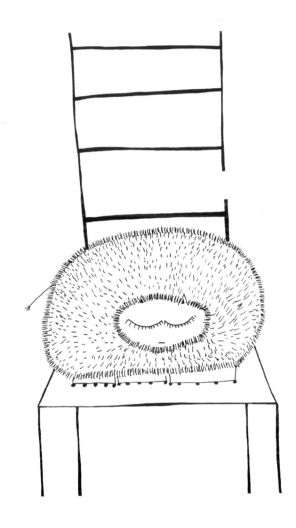

Next he was a porcupine
and he sat in chairs of people who were mean.

At last, Sandy dreamed he was a soft fluffy puppy.
And suddenly he woke up.
"That's silly," he said.
"That's the silliest thing I ever heard.
I am a puppy
and that's more fun than anything."

●

BELLS! BELLS! BELLS!

A bell on the clock
to open your eyes

A bell on the door
may be a surprise

A bell on the street
it could be a fire

Bells on the junk wagon
strung on a wire

A bell in your school
to start off your class

A typewriter bell
that tinkles like glass

A bell on the door
to welcome you in

A bicycle bell

One warm summer day, when there were many
children in the playground, Purkey the pigeon
had a very bad day. Purkey was having trouble
finding his lunch.

Other days he could find a cracker or a cookie dropped by some child...but not that day.

Purkey sat on a high branch over the picnic table between the swings and the seesaw and waited and waited.

Finally after a long while, a little baby just
learning to walk dropped his zwieback. The
baby's mother wouldn't let him pick it up from
the ground and eat it. But pigeons' mamas don't
care about such things so Purkey waited for them
to leave.

Meanwhile, he kept his eye on the zwieback.

As soon as they left, Purkey flew down.

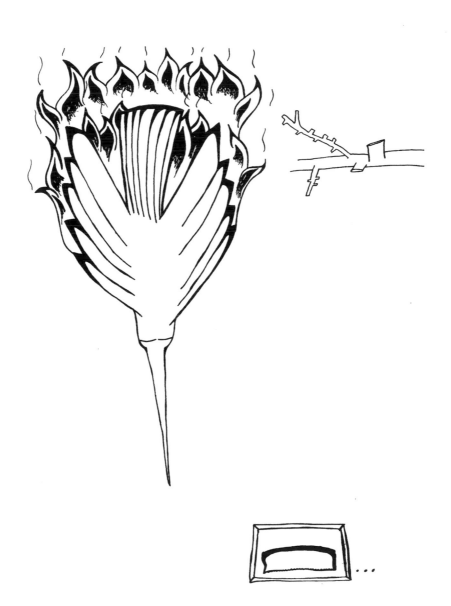

But just as he was about to peck at the zwieback, two boys dressed like cowboys ran by and scared him back to the branch.

So Purkey waited another little while and this time,
as he was about to fly down, a little girl came
skipping by with her jump rope.

When the little girl went away, a lady
with a baby buggy stopped right next
to the zwieback. Purkey knew they
wouldn't hurt him but he liked to be
alone when he was eating.

So he just sat and waited on his branch.

Purkey thought to himself, "Pretty soon I should
be able to eat in privacy." But no. Because when
the lady left, two little girls came by to play
hopscotch. And they played for the longest time.

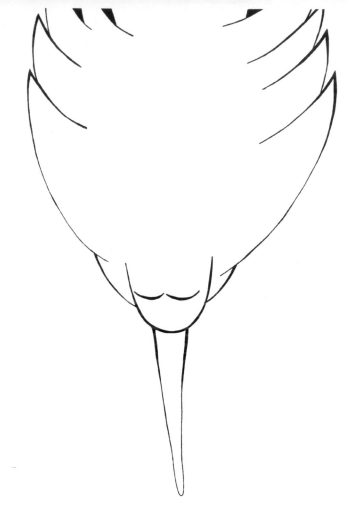

At last the game was over
and Purkey flew down once again.

This time, just as he was about to take a hungry
peck at the zwieback, a little boy with a stick
chased him back to the branch.

Purkey knew that children did this sometimes. But he thought the boy would go away soon.

Three times Purkey tried to eat his lunch and each time the little boy chased him away.

He had never had such a bad day.

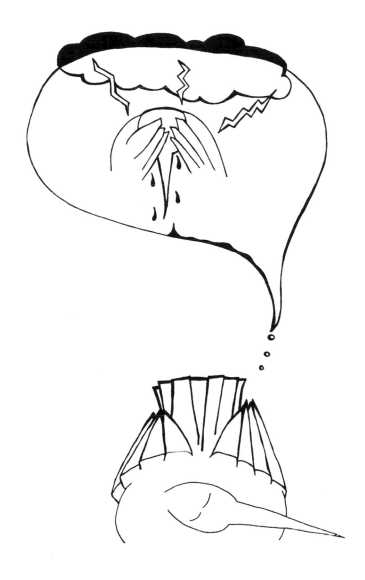

Purkey was so upset and so hungry, he wished he could cry, except that pigeons don't know how.

As he looked down from his branch he decided he would try just once more. This time, when he flew down the boy started to chase him again, but now his mother stopped him.

Purkey heard her tell the little boy that he should be a friend to pigeons and all the other birds.

She said,
"Look how nicely he
eats his lunch."

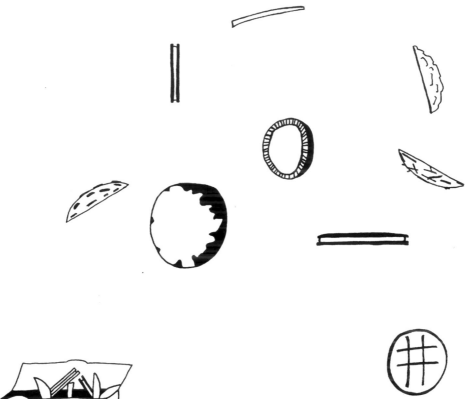

So they watched Purkey eat and the little boy enjoyed it so much, he got a box of cookies and threw some to him.

Purkey ate and ate until he felt just fine again.

Then he flew to his branch and looked down at his new friend. The boy was waving at him and offering him some more cookies.

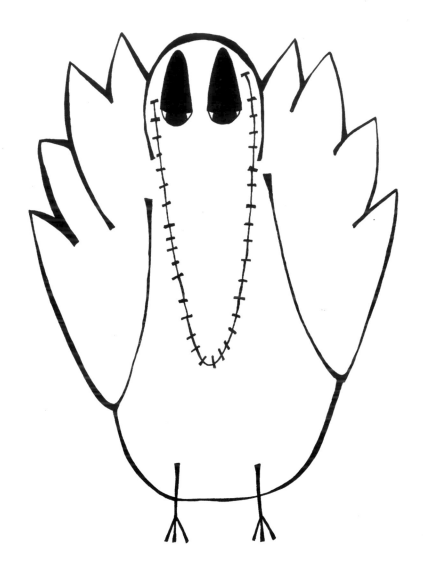

That made Purkey feel so good, he wished he could smile, except that pigeons don't know how to do that either.

And that was how a bad day became a very good day for Purkey.

●

If you should bite a lion
Your manners are the worst
That is unless of course
The lion bites you first.

Never pinch your tiger
Never punch your bear
Never drag your tortoise
Never pull your hare.

You do not need
An elephant's trunk
To know you're somewhere
Near a skunk.

To fill a kangaroo
    with gloom
Just call her pouch
    a kangaroom.

An aardvark
is no lark.
He doesn't bark
his home's no park.

He lives on ants
and just one glance
will show you that
he wears no pants.

The crocodile has scaly skin
and teeth much sharper than a pin.

He has four feet with ugly claws
instead of gentle furry paws.

His tail is long and hard and tough
I think I've gone quite far enough.

I think my friendship soon will end
I'll pick a rabbit for my friend.

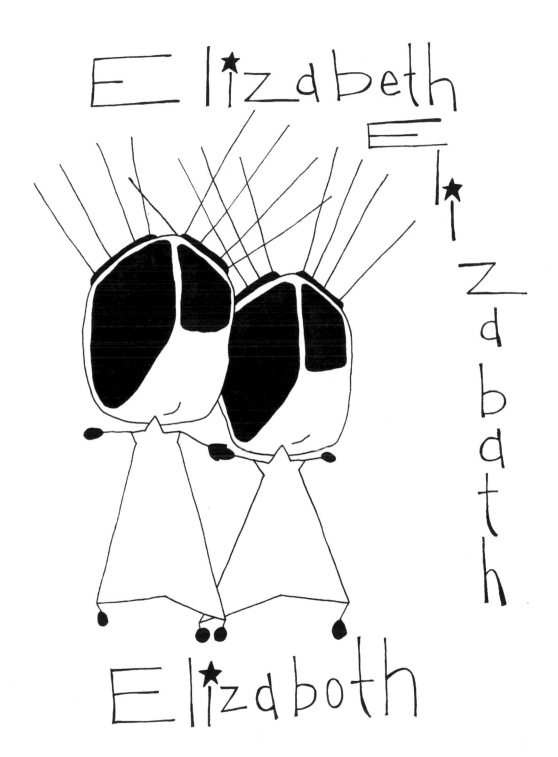

FUN WITH NAMES

Almost all first names can be changed a little bit
to sound more like the person you're talking about.
For instance:

ELIZABETH...when she is in the tub you could call her
Eliza**bath**. Or if there are two girls with that name,
they would be known as Eliza**both**.

DAVID...is all right in the daytime but after sunset
he should be called **Night**vid. When he is down the
street you might yell **Hey**vid.

PHILIP...when he's eating you could call him Phil**up**.
If he's getting fat he might be Phil**out**.

MARGARET...after dinner, we might refer to her as
Margar**ate**. If she takes after her father she might
be called **Pa**rgaret.

One sunny summer day
in the middle of winter
when the moon was shining
through the heavy dark clouds
the snow began to rain quite heavily.

Elizabeth looked through the window
but couldn't tell whether it was snaining or rowing.
All she could see was her own room.
But that was because she was outside.

"I better go in and look *out* the window
instead of looking *in* the window," she said,
"or I'll never know what the weather is supposed to be."

Someone was on the telephone
when she entered the room.
It was her best friend, named Elizabeth also,
(the daughter of Mr. and Mrs. Also.)

Most of the time the girls were known as Elizaboth.
And if one was in the tub she was called Elizabath.

"I can't talk to you now," Elizabeth told her. "I'm too late."
And she took her sled and started for school with her cat, Rover.

Rover thought he was a rooster
and would only say "Moo."
But since there was no place to roost,
he merely said "Quack."

Suddenly it began to rain—
but not too heavily.
It was only raining cats.
Or to be more exact—kittens.

Rover wanted to stay in the rain and make friends
but Elizabeth was in a hurry to get to school
before it started to rain lions.

They came to a bridge
and she took out a chalk to make a big X on it.
"There!" she said, "I crossed that one easily enough."
Then she wondered about the next one.
"Oh well," she told herself,
"I'll cross that bridge when I come to it."

Off in the distance
she saw what appeared to be
either a flying horse or a horse fly.
"Oh look!" Elizabeth cried, "Isn't that Uncle Harriet's
brown horse? Or is it a horse of another color?"
The only answer was a loud "neigh."

By this time
they came to the little red schoolhouse
which naturally was painted blue —
a house of another color.

She said, "Rover, you'll have to stay outside
because you have fleas.
Two is company but fleas a crowd."

So Rover bit her.
Then she bit back.
And bit by bit
they came to the school entrance.

And they were just in time
because her teacher, Miss Teacher,
was ringing the school bell.
It was an old cloth bell
which needed wringing
since she had just washed it in lukewarm water
(warmed by Luke, the school janitor.)

Off to one side of the school was a lot
with a few dogs in it barking loudly.
So Elizabeth put her bicycle in the barking lot,
rushed into the classroom and sat down.

"Hey," said a voice, "get off!
You're creasing my skin."
She had seated herself on Bossy,
the smartest pig in the class.

He was always raising his tail
to be the first to answer a question.

His ambition was to become a bank.
He hoped to grow a slot
in his head for pennies.

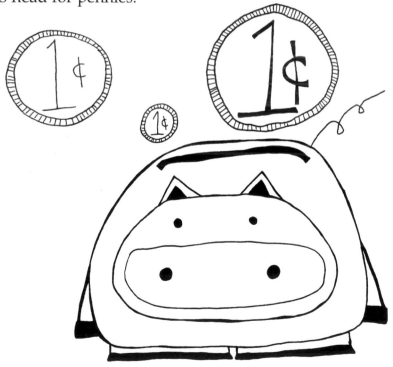

Bossy was forever trying
to get Elizabeth to give him a
girlyback ride.

"Haha," she laughed as she got off him.
"This time the tables are turned."
And sure enough several of the tables were turned
because she had entered in such a hurry.

Miss Teacher was under one of them
but she soon laughed it off.

Then climbing up on the chandelier,
she began.
"Our first lesson will deal with algebra."

Up went Bossy's tail.
"I can say 'how are you' in algebra," he shouted.

"Nonsense," said Miss Teacher.
"You can't *say* 'how are you' in algebra,
you have to sing it."
And she threw him a dirty look
which hit the wall
and broke into a million pieces.

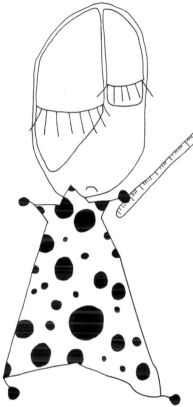

After they cleaned up the mess,
Miss Teacher asked,
"Where is Nicholas today?"
"Nicholas has measles," someone shouted.
"Oh yes. Sickolas," said Elizabeth
and everybody applauded.
Especially Elizabeth.

When the room quieted down,
they used the down to go to sleep on.
But the teacher woke them with,
"How about poetry?"
"No thanks, I just ate," Bossy answered.

"I have a poem by my father," Elizabeth
volunteered. And she began:

>"My eight-year old is noisy
>When she's in or out of doors
>And I would like to trade her
>For a quiet pair of fours."

"Very nice," said Miss Teacher.
"You say your father wrote the poem?"
"No," answered Elizabeth. "He typed it."

"I thought you were thirteen and not eight,"
the teacher said.
"That's true," Elizabeth answered.
"But my father couldn't find a rhyme for six and a half."

While the teacher was trying to figure that one out,
another voice spoke up.
It was Henry the Ninth.
He had hair that Elizabeth loved.
It was her own.
He had taken one of her pigtails
when her back was turned.

He was called Henry the Ninth
because his father wanted him to be a king
and was forever crowning him.
"My poem goes like this," Henry said.

> "Jack Spratt could eat no fat
> His wife could eat no lean
> And that is why all black berries
> Are always red when green."

"Beautiful," said Miss Teacher.
"But why do you think
the wife didn't like her meat too lean?"

"Because she wanted it to stand up straight,"
shouted Elizabeth.

But the teacher wasn't listening.
She was trying to find a rhyme for six and a half.
She was muttering to herself.
"Nix and a calf,
tricks and a laugh,
bix and a zaff,
kicks and giraffe."

Suddenly Bossy began to wave his tail so loudly,
Miss Teacher looked up.
Their conversation went something like this:

TEACHER: Yes? What is it?

BOSSY: What is what?

TEACHER: It!

BOSSY: It what?

TEACHER: Your tail.

BOSSY: What about my tail?

TEACHER: It was waving.

BOSSY: There must have been a draft.

TEACHER: Oh, I give up.

BOSSY: I didn't ask you a riddle.

TEACHER: All right. I'll ask *you* one.
          What can I hold that no one else can?

BOSSY: Your breath.

TEACHER: That's not fair, you pigged.
          I mean peeked.

Just then, the bell rang for lunch.
It was only eleven o'clock
but the bell got hungry early.

Henry the Ninth opened his lunch box.
There was a note inside.
It read:

YOU LEFT YOUR LUNCH HOME
LOSE TWENTY POINTS
AND MISS TWO TURNS.

Elizabeth looked into her own lunch box.
"Oh boy," she said,
"I have a sandwich made of real sand
and a whole cupful of elbow macaroni."

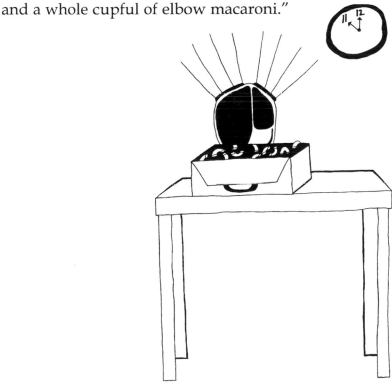

"Get your elbows off the table," Miss Teacher ordered angrily.
"I'm sorry," Elizabeth answered as she
looked around for a table to get her elbows off of.

But the only table she could see had no elbows on it.
It was loaded instead with knuckles—
pig's knuckles.
Bossy was having a little nap.

However his snoring was so loud,
it soon woke him up and
he went into the next room
to get away from the noise.

Meanwhile,
Miss Teacher put on her hat and coat
and started to leave.
"Where are you going?" Elizabeth asked her.
"I'm off to grandmother's house
to bring her some bakies I cooked,
cakies I booked, bookies I caked," she answered
and she climbed out the window.

"Is school over?" Elizabeth shouted after her.
"It certainly isn't under," Miss Teacher answered.
By that time she was already halfway into the woods
and heading for the nearest wolf.

So Elizabeth began putting her own coat on.
She did it slowly because it was difficult
while holding a cupful of elbow macaroni.

Suddenly she began to laugh.
"I'm not even supposed to be here.
Today is the other Elizabeth's turn for school.
They must have waked up the wrong girl."

●

I like one lump of sugar
in my little cup of tea
Some people might like two lumps
and someone might like three.

And so it is with animals
just like me and you
The dromedary likes one lump
the camel, he likes two.

●

If the boa constrictor stretched out flat
his tail would be a mile from his hat.

A mighty snake
is the boa constrictor
If he wrestled a lion
he'd be the victor.

●

The weasel is an awful sight
He lives on rats and vermin
But if you find his fur is white
then you can call him ermine.

I love the sound
of the merry-go-round
with its oomp de diddle de dee.

Oh the horns and the bells
of the old carousels
play the only music for me.

A calliope's great
and accordion's swell
But they just do not rate
with an old carousel.

So give me the sound
of the merry-go-round
with its oomp de diddle de dee.

As the horns and the bells
of the old carousels
play the only music for me.

The Tree
and Me

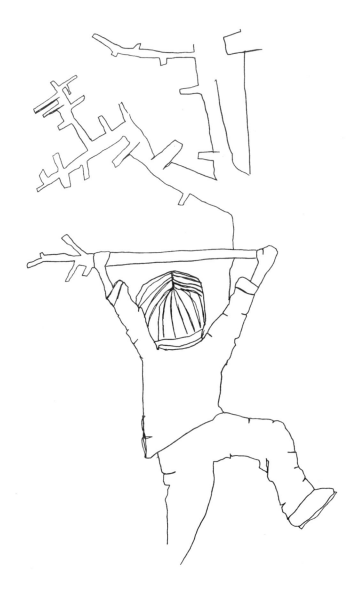

Eric looked around. Not a person or an animal
was in sight. Everything was very quiet. Even the
wind was still. He scrambled up the tree so
fast, it almost seemed as if he was climbing an
invisible ladder.

Up where the big branches start, Eric had a secret place for figuring things out. He went there now. Something was puzzling him. He sat down and leaned back against the tree to think.

I wish I could figure it out. I wish I could figure out which one is really me.

To my mother I'm still a little baby
who has to be watched
and fussed over all the time.

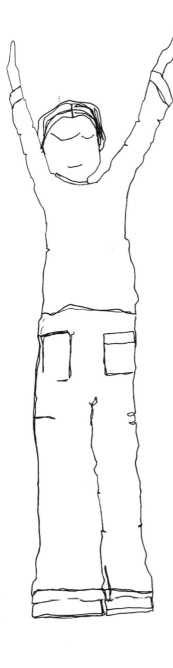

But my baby brother
thinks I'm a real grown-up.
He thinks I'm a giant.

My father says I'm very funny. He always laughs
at my jokes.

But my sister doesn't think I'm funny at all.
She says I'm just a mean brat and a pest.

To my teacher I'm the quiet boy in the third row.

But Mrs. Wersh, the lady downstairs, says I'm the noisiest kid on the block.

I wonder how I can figure out
who is right.

A warm breeze began to rustle the leaves
and Eric yawned.

I bet if I knew a hundred more people
there would be a hundred more ideas about me.

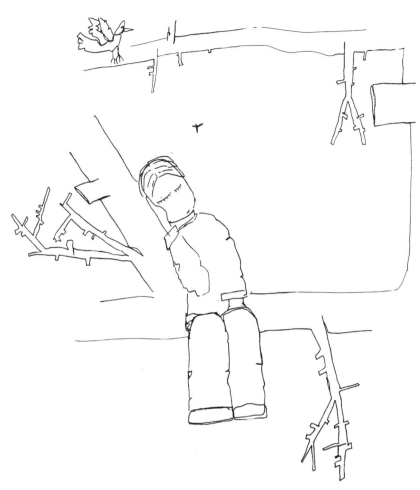

A bee buzzed overhead.

Even that bee probably has a different idea.
And that bird on the branch has another one.
He yawned again. I wonder who is right. I
wonder which one is me. He closed his eyes
to enjoy the warm breeze.

I wonder which one is me, I wonder which one is me, I wonder...
The words seemed to be saying themselves by now.

The leaves made a rustling noise again. It sounded like words. It sounded as if the tree was talking.

So you wonder which one is you? Well, everybody wonders about that. Me too. Even I wonder which one is me.

See that bee buzzing around. He thinks I'm just a place for the sweet nectar he gets from my blossoms. As far as he is concerned, I'm a soda fountain for bees.

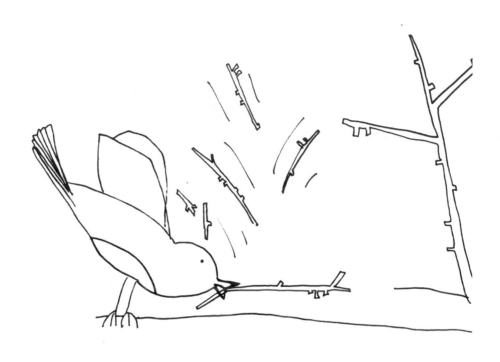

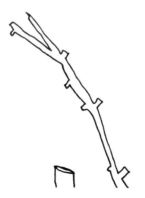

And that bird on the end of the branch. See him pulling out one of my dead twigs? Ouch! He comes here for supplies to build his nest. He thinks I'm a kind of lumber yard for birds.

Right over your head is a place in my trunk
where a squirrel has been staying. You can figure
out what he thinks. I'm just a squirrel apartment
house to him.

There's an inchworm right near your foot. He's
so busy chewing on one of my green leaves he
probably can't hear what I'm saying. To him,
I am an inchworm restaurant.

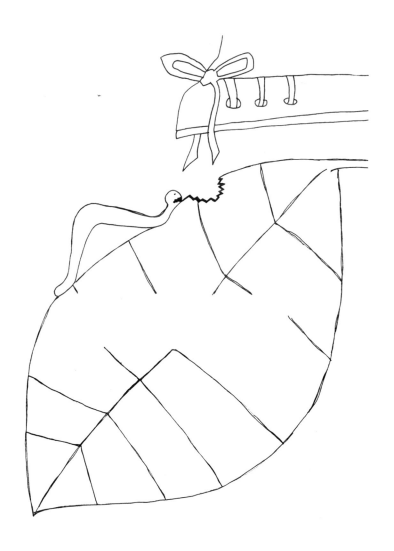

There are lots more. And each one has a different idea about me.

And everyone has a different idea about you too.

Your sister thinks you're a pest. Okay, maybe you are a pest to her. And maybe you are all those things the others think you are.

But the main thing is—you are you.

There are lots of boys and lots of trees.

But you're the only one of you and I'm the only one of me. See what I mean?

Eric thought about that for a minute. The wind had stopped blowing and the leaves became quiet as he sat there. He opened his eyes.

Say, that's right!

The tree is a lot of things, and so am I.

But mainly, no matter what anyone else thinks,

The tree is the tree—and I am me.

●

Here are things you must remember
Like there's no month that's called Octember.

It's hard to light a candle
At the bottom of the lake
Or gather any dewdrops
With a fish net or a rake.

Never put umbrellas
Under railroad trains
It's much too dark to see there
And it never, never rains.

The wind is very windy
The rain is very wet
This is the most peculiar summer
It hasn't snowed here yet.

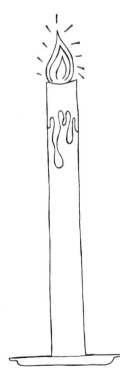

Here are things for you to know
And also good advice
Pushing over great big trucks
Isn't very nice.

Be careful when you cross the street
No matter where you are
You never know how you might meet
And damage someone's car.

It's very hard, you will agree
To be noisy quietly.

To wear your shoes upon your head
You're thinking with your feet instead.

When your hat's upon your feet
You will not be considered neat.

DID YOU KNOW you can find
WORDS INSIDE WORDS????
For example...
Inside of **DO**G
you can find **DO.**
Inside of C**AT**
you can find **AT.**

THERE ARE MANY WORDS
HIDDEN INSIDE OTHER WORDS.

LET'S SEE WHICH ONES WE CAN FIND...
If you look hard you'll see
there's an **OX** inside of B**OX**
and a **RAT** inside of C**RAT**E.

You might not be surprised
to find a **COT** inside of **COT**TAGE
or **US** in HO**US**E.

But imagine finding **TEN** in **TEN**T!

Here are some surprises.
If you look in B**OWL**
you can find **OWL**
and in S**INK**
there's **INK.**
Look in the **BAT**HTUB
and you'll find **BAT.**
In CUP**BOAR**D it may really surprise
you to find **BOAR**
and in **CORN**ER you have **CORN.**

108

Sometimes letters of a hidden word
are not next to each other
and have to be moved around.
For example:

In PA**CK**A**GE**
you can find **CAGE.**

If you look in **PR**ES**EN**T
you will find **PEN**

and **TA**B**LE** has **TALE.**

In these next words you will have to move
the letters around a little more.

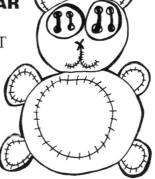

If you want to find **BEAR**
inside of **BAR**REL
and **CUB** in **BUC**KET

or to find **SKATE**
inside of B**ASKET**
and **CAT** in **AT**TIC.

Some words become other words by moving ALL
the letters around to form the new words.

SO

In **ART**
you can find **TAR**

and in **WORDS**
there is **SWORD.**

It's nice to know

in **ODOR** you can find **DOOR**
and in **SWING** you find **WINGS.**

But did you know

there's a **SHRUB** in **BRUSH**
or a **LUMP** in **PLUM**
or **HOSE** in **SHOE?**

We saved a surprise for the last.

In **ARMY** you can find **MARY!**

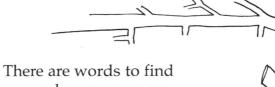

There are words to find
wherever you are.
Here are some you can find
if you are outside.

Of course there's **TREE**
in S**TREE**T

and **CUR**
in **CUR**B

and **RAIL**
in **LI**B**RA**RY

and **TUG**
in **GUT**TER.

But imagine finding **GOWN**
in **W**A**GON**

BOAT
in **AUT**OM**OB**ILE

DART
in HY**DRANT**

LAMB
in **MA**IL**B**OX

and **SEAL**
in B**ASE**BALL!

If you're at home, here are some things you might find:

A **WIND** in **WIND**OW.

And while you're there you might find

a **PIN** in RA**IN**DROP
or a **SNAKE** in **SN**OWFL**AKE.**

You know there is **NOISE** in TELEVI**SION**
and **AIR** in **RA**DIO.

But imagine finding **TOES** in CL**OSET**
or a **SOW** in **S**H**OW**ER
or a **GARTER** in REFRI**GERAT**OR!

You might even find **PEAR** in **CARPE**T
or **FRUIT** in **F**URN**ITUR**E.

And speaking of fruit...

Here are some of the things you can find in different fruit.

There's a **CAP** in **P**E**AC**H
and a **GEAR** in O**RANGE.**

A **LEMON** in WAT**ERMELON**
and **MOLE** in **LEMO**N.

CART in **A**P**RICOT**
and **APE** in **PEA**R.

Here's something interesting:

You can find a **PAL**
in **AP**P**L**E.

You can find **HER**
in C**HER**RY...

But to find **HIM**

see the next page.

In the animal world

you can find **HIM** in **CHIM**PANZEE.

In **TIG**E R you can find **TIE**.
In E**LEP**HAN T you can find **PLANE**.
In HIPPO**POT**AM**US** there is **SPOUT**.
In **CAM**EL there is **LACE**.
And in **WHAL**E there is **LAW!**

By this time you will not be surprised to find

OIL in **LIO**N
DOOR in C**ROC**OD**ILE**
MONEY in **MON**K**EY**
WASP in **SPA**RROW
NOOK in **K**ANGAR**OO**
FIRE in **GIR**AF**FE**
MAP in **P**UM**A**
LOAF in BUF**FALO**
SCORE in RHINO**CEROS.**

But although you can find **WOLF** in **FLOW**ER

that's really for the next page...

In the world of flowers

did you know there was **LOVE** in **VIOLE**T?
or **PIE** in **PE**TUNIA?

or for that matter a **ROSE** in H**ORSE?**

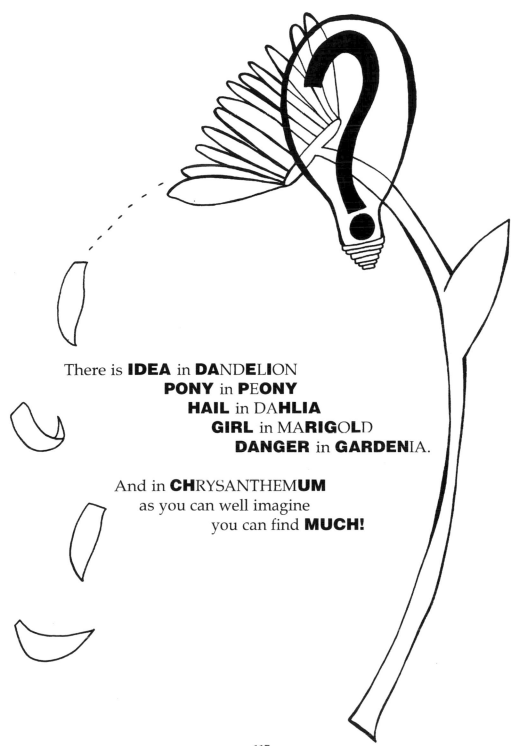

There is **IDEA** in **DA**ND**ELI**ON
PONY in **P**EONY
HAIL in DA**HLIA**
GIRL in MA**RIG**OLD
DANGER in **GARDEN**IA.

And in **CH**RYSANTHEM**UM**
as you can well imagine
you can find **MUCH!**

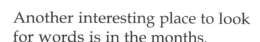

Another interesting place to look
for words is in the months.

For instance...

In JA**NUARY** you can naturally find **YARN.**
In F**EBRU**ARY you can find **FUR.**

You might find **RAM** in **MAR**CH
And you're likely to find **PAIL**
in **AP**R**IL.**

Imagine finding **MA** in **MA**Y
or the **UN** in **JUN**E.

In JULY you can't find anything! But
since JULY is named after JULIUS CAESAR
we can look inside of J**UL**I**US...**
and find **SULU** (a Filipino native).

There's **GAS** in A**U**G**US**T
and **PETS** in **SEPT**EMBER.
OCTOBER has **BOOT**
and N**OVEM**BER has **MOVER**
and good old **DE**CEMB**ER** has **DEER.**

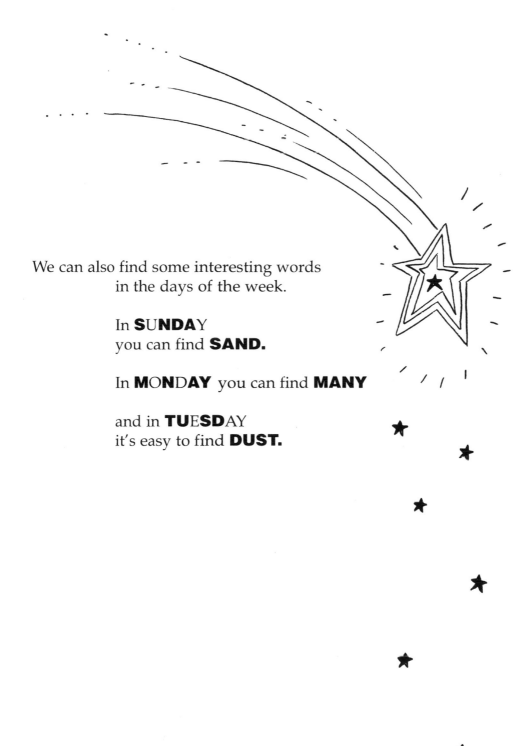

We can also find some interesting words
in the days of the week.

In **SUNDA**Y
you can find **SAND.**

In **MONDA**Y you can find **MANY**

and in **TUESD**AY
it's easy to find **DUST.**

WED**NESDA**Y
has **SEDAN.**

There is **TRAY**
in **T**HU**R**SD**AY**

and **FAIRY**
in **FRI**D**AY.**

SATU**R**DAY
has **STAR.**

In some words you can find MANY
different words.

For instance...

In **OCEAN** you can find
all of these:

ONE

   CONE

      CANE

        CAN

          ACE

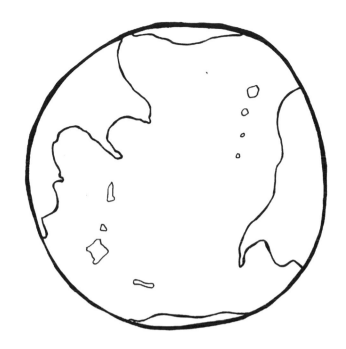

And in **EARTH** there is

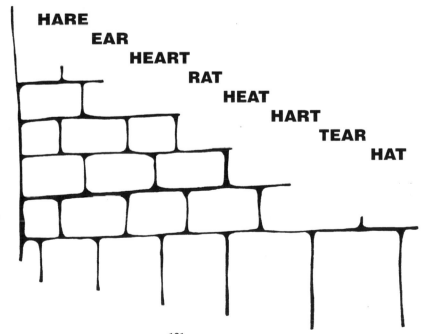

HARE
EAR
HEART
RAT
HEAT
HART
TEAR
HAT

All over the world there
are words to find.

Let's examine some countries...

In **FRANCE** there is **CAFE**
and in AR**GEN**T**INA** there is **GIANT.**
BEL**GIUM** has **GUM**
and in **I**RE**LAN**D you find **NAIL.**
In W**ALES** you will find **SEA**
and in **ENGLA**ND there is **GALE.**
H**OLL**AND has **DOLL**
and **CH**I**LE** has **ICE.**
CHINA has **INCH**
and **MEXIC**O has **MICE.**

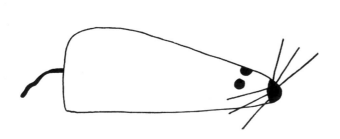

You can find **COLT** in S**COTL**AND
MARE in D**ENMAR**K
and **PURR** in P**U**ER**TO** **R**ICO.

There's **LARIAT** in A**USTRALIA**
and **WAND** in NEW ZEAL**AND.**

In CA**NAD**A you'll find **AND**
and in **LAOS, ALSO.**

How about trying to find out
what is in your name?

Or in your friend's name?

You might find some of these...

There's **SAIL** in ME**LIS**SA
and **OGRE** in **ROGE**R.

There is **FERN** in JENNI**FER**
     CLAM in **MI**CH**A**E**L**
        and **COAL** in **CA**R**OL.**

There's **DARN** in **ARN**OL**D**
     HORSE in CHRIS**TO**P**HER**
        TOY in TIM**OT**H**Y**
       DIN in **D**EN**NI**S
        and **KEY** in **KE**RR**Y.**

And you can find...
     YES in **S**HELLE**Y, NO** in J**OH**N
       and **MAYBE** in **MAYBE**LLE.

125

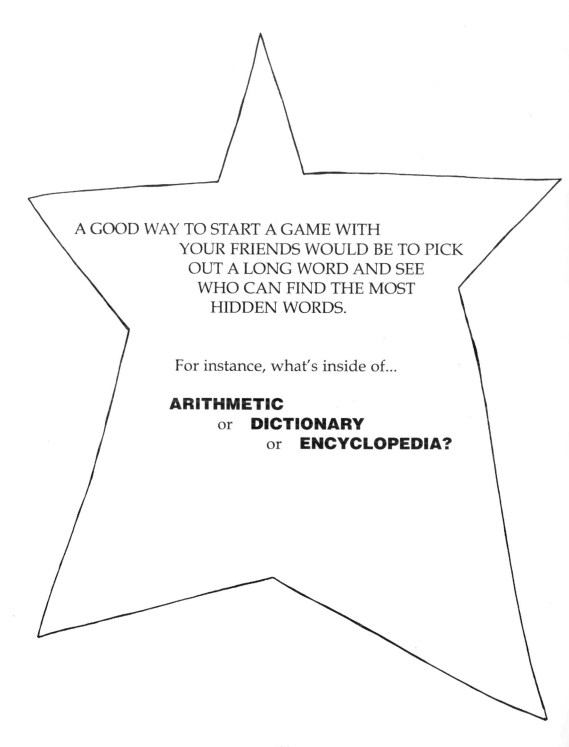

A GOOD WAY TO START A GAME WITH
YOUR FRIENDS WOULD BE TO PICK
OUT A LONG WORD AND SEE
WHO CAN FIND THE MOST
HIDDEN WORDS.

For instance, what's inside of...

ARITHMETIC
or **DICTIONARY**
or **ENCYCLOPEDIA?**

OF COURSE
YOU COULD STOP AT ANY PAGE IN
THIS BOOK AND USE IT TO START A GAME.

Now here's something that may
surprise you...

Look what you find inside of

'INSIDE'?

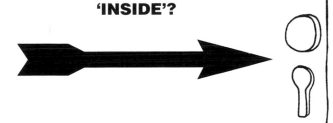

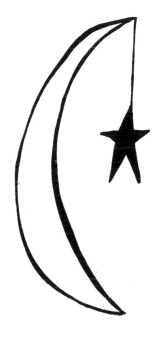

Everybody's lost balloon
Must be resting on the moon.

In the daytime in the light
I'm my mother's star
But at night when day is done
I'm my father's son.

Don't race the moon
Whatever you do.
'Cause he will go
As fast as you.

Careful Carlos was sent on an errand.
His mother told him to go down to the
corner market and buy a quart of milk.

"Milk is very refreshing on a warm day like
this," she told Carlos.

In the market down at the corner were
stands selling all kinds of meats, fruits, and
dairy foods, as well as dishes and other
things.

Carlos walked along until he came to a
stand selling milk. He stopped in front of it.

"Good morning," the stout man behind the
counter said, "I see you're looking for milk.
A glass of milk on a day like today is as
refreshing as a slice of watermelon."

"Watermelon! Maybe Mama would like watermelon even better," Carlos said to himself.

He turned away and walked a few steps to where a large glass case held a half of a watermelon and a few large slices. He stood looking at the watermelon for a while, licking his lips.

"Isn't that beautiful watermelon?" the man behind the counter asked. "It's as red as beefsteak. And it tastes good, too."

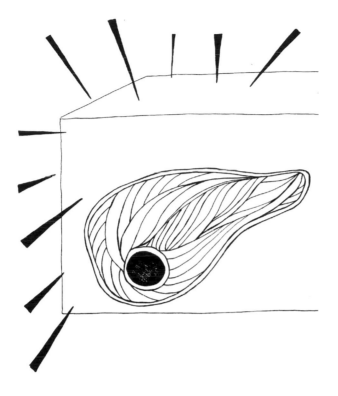

But Carlos had already turned away to go to the butcher's stall. He looked up at the man in the white apron.

"Is that beefsteak?" he asked, pointing at a large piece of meat in the gleaming white case. "Yes it is," the man answered, "and it's as tender as a plum. Say, where are you going?"

For on hearing the butcher's words, Carlos was on his way to the fruit stand. It was piled high with rows of delicious-looking apples, peaches, pears, oranges, plums, and grapes. He reached out to touch one of the plums.

"Be careful there!" the fruit man called out to him. "Don't squeeze the plums. They will lose their juice. And the juice is as sweet as honey."

Honey! Carlos remembered he had passed
the stand earlier. He ran back to it. There
they were, jars of beautiful honey piled high.

The lady behind the counter smiled at him.
"Would you care for some honey?" she asked.
"As you can see, it's as clear as crystal."

As the lady spoke the last word, Carlos looked across the way at the stand with all the glasses and bowls. He walked over to it slowly. One of the bowls gleamed in the light, and he went closer to look at it.

"It's as pretty as rock candy, isn't it?" said the man behind the counter.

Carlos nodded as he turned away to the candy counter. In a corner of the case were bags of sparkling rock candy.

Carlos was about to buy a bag when the candy lady said, "All our candy is as fresh as newly laid eggs."

Carlos was off like a shot to the egg counter.

"These eggs have yolks as yellow as butter," the lady behind the counter said. "How many do you want?"

Careful Carlos didn't hear her question.
He was at the next stand looking at the
butter.

"Buy your butter here," called the man.
"Fresh butter! Butter as smooth as maple
syrup. Buy your butter here!"

By now Carlos was on his way to the maple syrup counter.

The lady there saw him coming over and asked, "Would you like some maple syrup? It's as pure as milk."

Careful Carlos walked back to the milk
stand.

"Good morning," the stout man behind the
counter said, "Would you like some milk?

A glass of milk on a day like today is
as refreshing as..."

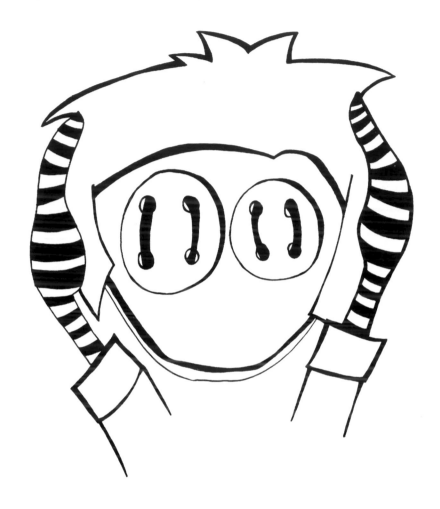

But Careful Carlos had his hands over his ears. *"Please, just give me a quart of milk,"* he said.

"Here is the milk, Mama," said Carlos
when he got home.

"I knew I could depend on you," said his
mother.

● Many kinds of words are wrong
Like shortbread when it's made too long.

Or peanuts which don't taste like peas
Or china which is Japanese.

To pour drinks from a bottle
You should remove the cork.

And when you are having soup
Don't use a knife and fork.

Ketchup, salt, pepper, mustard
Aren't very good in custard.

Yummy is the word for mustard
But it's phooey when on custard.

If You Talked To A Boar

If a tree was **BARE...**

Would it look like a **BEAR?**

If you had a **HARE...**

Would he comb his **HAIR?**

If you sat on a **STAIR...**

Would you sit and **STARE?**

If you lost your **BALL...**

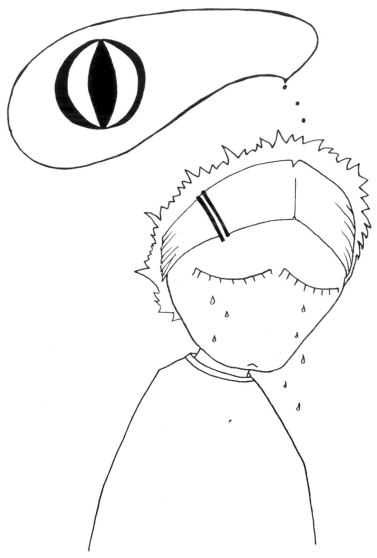

Would it make you **BAWL?**

If you talked to a **BOAR**...

Would he be a **BORE?**

If you had a **EWE...**

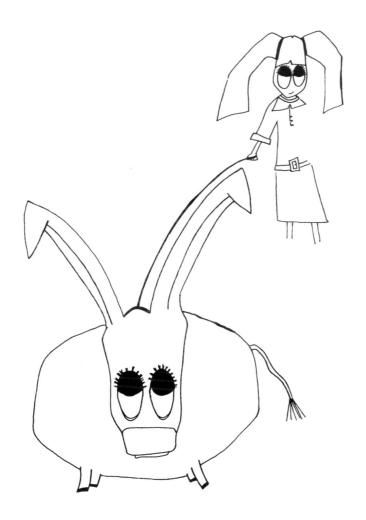

Would it look like **YOU?**

If you had two **GNUS...**

Would they read the **NEWS?**

If you really **BLEW...**

Would you turn real **BLUE?**

If a cat was on your **SHOE...**

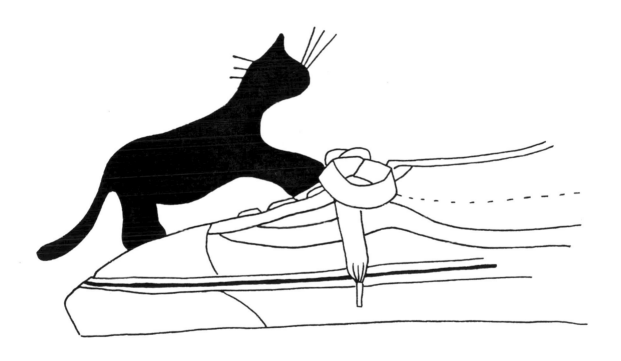

Would you yell **SHOO?**

And **last...** but not **least...**

If you waited for **DAYS...**

Would you be in a **DAZE?**

If you waited a **WEEK...**

Would you be very **WEAK?**

If you waited a **NIGHT...**

Would you be a good **KNIGHT?**

GOOD NIGHT

● If you should eat
A rhino's feet
A goldfish bowl
A doughnut hole
Two live frogs
A pair of clogs
A pound of chalk
A parrot's squawk
A tiger's tail
An old tin pail
A plaster wall
A rubber ball
Then mighty quick
You might get sick.

● The platypus is built so queer
it's a trial to conceive it.

I'd like to tell you how he looks
but you never would believe it.

They say that he's a mammal
(that means like you or me)

or an elephant or camel
or a squirrel in a tree.

But he looks so darn peculiar
with his web feet and his bill.

He looks like cousin Julia
or else like Uncle Bill.

● Clams really are just shellfish
When they're stingy then they're selfish.

One thing that I will always tell fish
Is stingy clams are selfish shellfish.

● The rhino, though his eyes are weak
has much more hide than I would seek.

The rhinoceros is gentle but...
He never looks for trouble but...

He isn't very mental but...
Don't let him near or he will
                    BUTT!!

● The rattlesnake is very mean
He's always ready to do battle.

His poisoned fangs are very sharp
His tail's a very scary rattle.

But you can tell when he is near
Because the rattle, it'll tattle.

WHAT'S THE BIGGEST WORD YOU KNOW?

The biggest word I know or can find in any dictionary is

FLOCCINAUCINIHILIPILIFICATION.

It is easier to pronounce than it looks. Just do it slowly, like this:

FLOCK-SEE-

       NAW-SEE-

              NYE-HILLI-

                    PILLI-

                        FIC-AY-SHUN

After practicing it a few times you should be able to say it easily. Try it and amaze your friends. Floccinaucinihilipilification means criticism of things or people in such a way as to make them seem unimportant. If someone should say "Oh that isn't much of a book" they are floccinaucinihilipilificating.

As I said before, that's the biggest word I could find. If you find a bigger one, please send it to me.

Of course some people say the biggest word is **RUBBER** because it can be stretched.

Or that the biggest is **SMILES** because there is a mile between the first and last letters.

A word that is not only big but also interesting is

ONOMATOPOEIA (AH-NO-MAT-O-<u>PEE</u>-A).

It is the name for words which sound like the noises they are describing. For example, these words for loud noises:

BANG!　　**CRASH!**　　**CLANG!**

Or these for noises that are not quite so loud:

CRUNCH　　**CLINK**　　**POP**

Or these for noises that are even softer:

BUZZ　　**WHIRR**　　**SWISH**

And how about these?

> The **crack** of a bat.
> The **snap** of a whip.
> The **whoosh** of a racing car.
> The **woof-woof** of a dog.
> The **splash** of water.

A small dictionary could be written just for words with onomatopoeia.

Here are some other examples:

The word for the sound of bells is
TINTINNABULATION (TIN-TIN-AB-YOU-<u>LAY</u>-SHUN).   That
includes **ring, clang, bong, jingle, jangle** and many more.

And there is a special word for a whispering sound.
It is **SUSURRUS** (SOO-<u>SOOR</u>-US). It sounds like the wind blowing
through the dry leaves on the trees.

There is a whole set of words which end with NYM. Words like:

HOMONYM

SYNONYM

ANTONYM

PSEUDONYM

ACRONYM

A **HOMONYM** (<u>HAH</u>-MO-NIM) is the kind of word which sounds like another word but is spelled differently and has another meaning. Like **PEAR** and **PAIR** or **TWO** and **TOO**. Or **NIGHT** and **KNIGHT** or **WEEK** and **WEAK**. As you can tell, these are words to have fun with. Or maybe I should have said, to have pun with, because most of our puns are homonyms.

A **SYNONYM** (<u>SIN</u>-OH-NIM) is a word that means the same as another word. Words such as **PAIR** and **COUPLE** are synonyms. So are **STOUT** and **FAT**.

An **ANTONYM** (<u>ANT</u>-OH-NIM) is a word that has the opposite meaning. **BLACK** and **WHITE** are antonyms. So are **RICH** and **POOR**. If you were to put your finger in front of a crawling ant, he would probably turn and go the <u>opposite</u> way. That could be your mnemonic for remembering that an **ANTONYM** is a word of the <u>opposite</u> meaning.

A **PSEUDONYM** (<u>SOO</u>-DOE-NIM) is an artificial or fictitious name, like Mark Twain, which is the pseudonym for the famous author's real name, Samuel Clemens. Another word for pseudonym is **PEN NAME** or as the French say it, **NOM DE PLUME**. One of England's greatest novelists, Mary Anne Evans is better known by her pseudonym George Eliot. And El Greco was the pseudonym of one of the world's great masters of painting whose real name was Domenikos Theotokopoulos.

A word that everybody should know is **ACRONYM** (<u>ACK</u>-ROE-NIM). An acronym is a name made out of the first letters of a series of words. Like **UNICEF** for the **U**nited **N**ations **I**nternational **C**hildren's **E**mergency **F**und. Or **NASA** for the **N**ational **A**eronautics and **S**pace **A**dministration.

We are surrounded by **ACRONYMS** these days.

Here are some others you may have heard about:

SCUBA   **S**elf-**C**ontained **U**nderwater **B**reathing **A**pparatus.

LASER   **L**ight **A**mplication through **S**timulated **E**mission of **R**adiation. Everyone will agree it's much easier just to say **LASER**.

NATO   **N**orth **A**tlantic **T**reaty **O**rganization.

ACRONYMS can make it easy to remember things. For instance, here is a two-word acronym which provides a simple way to remember the offices of the cabinet of the United States. The acronym is **HALT DISPATCH**. Each letter stands for a different office. Like this:

Health **E**ducation and **W**elfare
(which is known by its own acronym **HEW**)

    Agriculture
    Labor
    Treasury

    Defense
    Interior
    State
    Postmaster General
    Attorney General
    Transportation
    Commerce
    Housing and **U**rban **D**evelopment (known by its acronym **HUD**)

And that brings us to the interesting word

MNEMONIC (NEM-<u>ON</u>-IC).

Any device like an acronym which can help you to remember things is called a **MNEMONIC**. Some people tie a string on a finger to use as a mnemonic. But very often they forget what it was they had to remember.

Many of the words in our language come from the names of people. One example is the word

SPOONERISM (<u>SPOON</u>-ER-ISM).

A Spoonerism is a sentence in which the words get twisted. It is named for William Spooner the head of an English College who often twisted his sentences when speaking. Once when he wanted to say "a half-formed wish" he said instead "a half-warmed fish." Another time when he was going to tell certain pupils that they had wasted two whole terms, it came out as "you have tasted two whole worms."

Next in our parade of interesting words is

PALINDROME (PAL-IN-DROME).

See if you can tell what palindromes are. Here are some examples:

BOB   **RADAR**   **PUP**

DAD   **NOON**   **PEEP**

ABLE WAS I ERE I SAW ELBA

MADAM I'M ADAM

If you didn't know it before, you know now that a palindrome is a word or sentence that reads the same forward or backward. Try making up a palindrome of your own.

And you might also try your hand at

ALLITERATION (AL-LIT-ER-AY-SHUN).

This describes a phrase or name made up of a series of words most of which start with the same letter. One of the best-known alliterations is the one that goes:

Peter Piper picked a peck of pickled peppers.
Where's the peck of pickled peppers Peter Piper picked?

This phrase is also a **TONGUE TWISTER**, which is another alliteration. If Peter Piper is easy for you to speak, try saying Baby Buggy Bumpers very fast three times in a row.

But not all alliterations are tongue twisters. Some examples are: Herbert Hoover, Mickey Mantle or American Automobile Association.

And not all tongue twisters are alliterations. For example: A box of biscuits; a box of mixed biscuits; and a biscuit mixer. Try saying those phrases fast.

OXYMORON (OX-EE-<u>MORE</u>-ON) is another very special word. It is a phrase in which two words of opposite meaning are used together. For example, in order to be funny or dramatic, a writer might talk about a **LOUD SILENCE** or a **BURNING COLD** or a **CRUEL KINDNESS**. In ordinary conversation we sometimes use an **OXYMORON** accidentally by saying, "That picture is **PRETTY UGLY**" or asking "Isn't that coat a **LITTLE BIG** for you?"

One word which is only for very special use is

DEFENESTRATION (DEE-FEN-ESS-<u>TRAY</u>-SHUN).

It means "the act of throwing something out of the window."
The word **DEFENESTRATION** is not very much in use mainly because people do not do much throwing of things out of the window these days fortunately. But just in case anybody should ever think of doing such a thing, you will know it's called **DEFENESTRATION**.

This book started with the biggest word I could find.
Now, here at the end, is a big word which means "a big word."

SESQUIPEDALIAN

SESS-
            KWEE-
                        PED-
                                    AY-
                                                LEE-
                                                            AN

Sesquipedalian also has another definition. It means "a foot and a half long." You could say that **SESQUIPEDALIAN** is a sesquipedalian.

About the author:

Michael Sage (1912-1995) was an actor on Broadway and radio. He was a professional writer. He taught classes in public speaking and remedial English for the New York City Department of Personnel. In Philadelphia, he did public relations for non-profits and a regular column carried by a number of regional publications. Seven of his books for children were published between 1966 and 1970. Six of them are included in this volume (Dippy Dos and Don'ts, Deep in a Haystack, The Tree and Me, Words Inside Words, Careful Carlos, and If You Talked to a Boar), as well as three works never published before now.

About the artist:

Jenny Ross (b. 1975) graduated from Tyler School of Art, Temple University, in 1998. She taught art to children ages 6 through 15. She is also a painter and writes and illustrates her own comic books.

About the publisher:

Joan Sage: Mike was Joan's soulmate for 31 and a half years. Putting together this book was a labor of love.

Also by Michael Sage:

ONE GOOD FRIEND (ISBN 0-9669813-0-8)

Responses when ONE GOOD FRIEND (126 pages, without illustrations) was originally published (1968 hardcover by Cobble Hill Press):

"...children's classic...of literary merit...action and characterization to attract both the reluctant and the avid reader...well characterized, highly sympathetic hero to whom urban children...or any children...should respond with empathy."
> —Office of Curriculum, Bureau of English, Board of
>   Education of the City of New York.

"...the theme is one which all youth have felt at one time or another and which they can relate to..."
> —Dept. of Public Instruction, State of Wisconsin.

"...found the story absorbing and direct. The emotional impact of it is tremendous."
> —Dept. of Public Instruction,
>   Commonwealth of Pennsylvania.

"The story is fast moving and keeps one wondering what is coming next."
> —Dept. of Education, Commonwealth of Kentucky.

Speaking of ONE GOOD FRIEND, Michael Sage said: "Most of us have endured a feeling of loneliness at some time in our lives. In big cities especially, it is easy to feel like a hungry wanderer looking through the window at the rest of the world enjoying a feast. I set out to write a story about that feeling for everyone who has ever been lonely."

The plot of ONE GOOD FRIEND is deceptively simple: a lonely boy meets a lonely wolf at the zoo. A bond between them is woven, strand by strand. But the comings and goings of the characters are merely vehicles to convey a much more profound message: the ache of loneliness, the need for all life to seek closeness, loyalty and unity with its own kind. The author has caught a glimpse of these universals and maintained his insight from first page to last. The result is a story told with disarming directness and understatement which has an astonishing emotional impact. Michael Sage lets us enter the heart of a young boy who stirs echoes of our own youth and of our needs for friendship and devotion.

ONE GOOD FRIEND (ISBN 0-9669813-0-8)
republished in paperback in 1999, can be obtained (as well as "THE WHIMSICAL SAGE") by contacting the publisher, Joan Sage, 914 Kimball Street, Philadelphia, PA 19147.